FAMOUS IMMIGRANT
COMPUTER
SCIENTISTS

MAKING AMERICA GREAT
IMMIGRANT SUCCESS STORIES

FAMOUS IMMIGRANT
COMPUTER
SCIENTISTS

Donna M. Bozzone, PhD

Enslow Publishing
101 W. 23rd Street
Suite 240
New York, NY 10011
USA

enslow.com

Published in 2018 by Enslow Publishing, LLC.
101 W. 23rd Street, Suite 240, New York, NY 10011

Library of Congress Cataloging-in-Publication Data

Names: Bozzone, Donna M., PhD
Title: Famous immigrant computer scientists / Donna M. Bozzone, PhD
Description: New York : Enslow Publishing, 2018. | Series: Making America great: immigrant success stories | Includes bibloigraphical references and index. | Audience: Grades 7–12.
Identifiers: ISBN 9780766092464 (library bound) | ISBN 9780766095922 (paperback)
Subjects: LCSH: Computer scientists—United States—Biography—Juvenile literature. | Immigrants—United States—Juvenile literature.
Classification: LCC QA76.2.A2 B69 2018 | DDC 004.092/2 [B]—dc23

Printed in the United States of America

Contents

Introduction

The United States is a nation of immigrants. With the exception of Native Americans, everyone in the country is an immigrant or descendant of those who came to the United States from elsewhere—either by choice or force.

The diversity that immigration has produced in America drives the engine of creativity nationwide. By taking a closer look at how people from all over the world have made the United States the country it is today, it's easy to see that the contributions of immigrants are just as important as those of native-born Americans. Consider this small sampling of the many immigrants who've left their mark on the United States:

- E. J. du Pont (France): founder of DuPont, one of the largest chemical companies in the world
- Maxwell Kohl (Poland): founder of Kohl's department stores
- Sol Shenck (Russia): founder of Big Lots! discount store chain
- Charles Pfizer (Germany): founder of Pfizer, one of the world's biggest pharmaceutical firms
- John W. Nordstrom (Sweden): founder of Nordstrom, a chain of luxury department stores

Immigrants even founded companies so familiar to most Americans that they seem to be part of US history: AT&T, RadioShack, Kraft Foods, Colgate, and Sara Lee.

Immigrants have especially played a role in the growth and development of computer technology. This book explores five such people: Sundar Pichai, Sergey Brin, Pierre Omidyar, Lisa Su, and Jan Koum. Each of these computer scientists has made a difference not only in what they have helped to invent but also in their contributions to society.

Computer technology touches the lives of people in numerous ways. Here, a teacher is helping adults learn to speak and read English. These adults immigrated to the United States from many countries. Mastering English will make life easier for them.

The number of important computer scientists and engineers who've come to the United States from overseas far outnumber the five described in the chapters that follow. In fact, several books could be written about the influential role of immigrants in the growth of American technology. Here are just a few examples:

- Elon Musk (South Africa): inventor of the Tesla car and founder of PayPal
- Jordi Muñoz (Mexico): developer of drone aircraft
- Vinod Khosla (India): cofounder of Sun Microsystems
- Andrew Grove (Hungary): founder of Intel
- Miguel de Icaza (Mexico): software developer for Microsoft
- Jerry Yang (Taiwan): cofounder of Yahoo!, one of the first web browsers that allowed people to search the internet
- Satya Nadella (India): CEO of Microsoft
- Ruchi Sanghvi (India): the first female computer engineer hired by Facebook
- David Hindawi (Iraq): cofounder of the cybersecurity firm Tanium

The overall contribution that immigrants make to the tech industry is jaw dropping. More than half of the people who have created high-tech startup companies in Silicon Valley, California, (the center of the industry) have been immigrants. Also, immigrants have launched 25 percent of the engineering and technology startups in the nation. In 2006, 40 percent of all patent applications filed in the United States were from inventors born in foreign countries.

And that's not all. Immigrants make up a large percentage of the graduate-level science and technology workforce. They represent 48 percent of workers with chemistry master's degrees, 56 percent with software engineer master's degrees, as well as 63 percent of doctoral-level engineers and 64 percent of doctoral-level software and electrical engineers.

The contributions of immigrants and foreign nationals to science and technology in the United States are enormous. It is clear that they are the fuel that keeps us going in the Information Age.

Now that you have a sense of the broad influence immigrants have in the American tech world, zoom in on the stories of five computer scientists in particular who have made a difference.

CHAPTER 1

SUNDAR PICHAI: THE CEO OF GOOGLE

On January 27, 2017, President Donald Trump issued an executive order banning citizens from seven majority-Muslim nations from entering the United States. These countries are: Syria, Iran, Sudan, Libya, Somalia, Yemen, and Iraq. Before federal judges ultimately blocked the travel ban, it sparked a reaction from many executives, scientists, and engineers in high tech. Sundar Pichai, chief executive officer (CEO) of Google, said that at least 187 employees at the company would be affected by the ban.

"We're upset about the impact of this order and any proposals that could impose restrictions on Googlers and their families, or that could create barriers to bringing great talent to the US," he told the staff. "It is painful to see the personal cost of this executive order on our colleagues. Our first order of business is to help Googlers who are affected."[1]

Why did Sundar Pichai react so strongly to the travel ban? He does not come from one of the affected countries, but many of his employees do. Moreover, Pichai himself is an immigrant. Now an American citizen, he was born in India but has contributed tremendously to his new homeland. From his personal experience, he knows that most immigrants to the United States come to the country to make a good life and share their talents. Let's take a look at Pichai's life and see how he joined the American family.

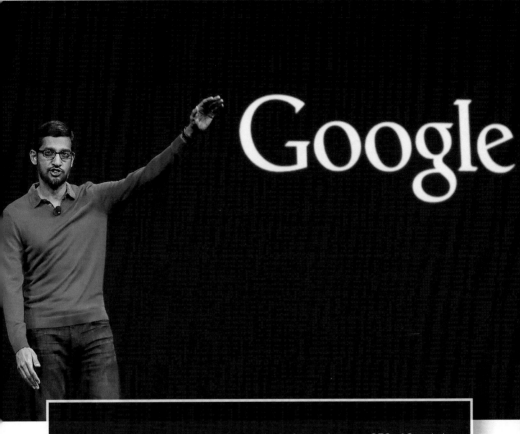

Sundar Pichai is shown here a few months before he became CEO of Google in 2015. He is delivering a presentation at Google's annual conference.

EARLY LIFE

Born in 1972 in Chennai, a city of seven million people in the southern Indian state of Tamil Nadu, Sundar Pichai grew up in a household missing the conveniences Americans take for granted. His family had a two-room apartment; Sundar and his younger brother slept in the living room. The family had no telephone until Sundar was twelve years old. They had neither a television nor a car. The family either

Sundar Pichai grew up in Chennai, India. Although his family was not wealthy and lived modestly, Chennai is a city that attracts affluent visitors. Its beautiful beaches are one of the reasons people travel to Chennai.

used the bus for transportation or all four of them—parents, Sundar, and his brother—piled onto the family's small scooter.

Sundar's parents were hardworking and sacrificed to provide for their sons. His mother, Lakshmi, was a stenographer before having children, and his father, Regunatha, was an electrical engineer for the British company GEC. He managed a factory that made electrical parts and often discussed his job with his son.

"I used to come home and talk to him a lot about my work day and the challenges I faced," he said. "Even at a young age, he was curious about my work. I think it really attracted him to technology."[2]

Sundar's grandmother remembers him as a curious boy who was eager to learn. "He used to play cricket with friends but never let it affect his studies," she said. "He hated wasting time."[3] His school friends recall him as shy, quiet, nerdy, and studious. Pattu Subramanian, two years ahead of Sundar in school, said that he used to have a smile on his face and (was) kind of a bookworm.

13

CHENNAI, INDIA

Once called Madras, Chennai is a port city located on the Coromandal Coast off the Bay of Bengal. More than seven million people live in the borders of the city, and nearly two million more live in the surrounding areas. Its large population has helped give Chennai one of the largest economies of any Indian city. Automobile manufacturing is one of its strongest industries. The city boasts numerous museums and galleries as well as music, theater, and dance establishments. Chennai also houses many major film studios. With beautiful temples, historical and cultural sites, and beaches, it's no surprise that Chennai is one of the most popular tourist destinations in India.

According to schoolmate Srividhya Sainathan, "He was passionate about math and science, and had a tight circle of friends equally focused on academics."[4] Another schoolmate remembers Sundar as "a devoted son to his parents."[5] And cousin Aravind Vasudevan described Sundar as highly intelligent, but also loving, down to earth, and very respectful to elders.

EDUCATION AND THE MOVE TO THE UNITED STATES

Sundar began his education at Jawahar Vidylaya, a school that included the first through tenth grades. Academically talented, Sundar was accepted to the Indian Institute of Technology Kharagpur where he studied metallurgical engineering. His work at IIT Kharagpur was so outstanding that he won a scholarship to attend Stanford University to study materials science and semiconductor physics. Semiconductors are key parts of most electronic circuits.

A SOURCE OF TECHNOLOGISTS FOR THE WORLD

What do the following individuals, all successes in the high-tech industry, have in common?

- N. R. Narayana Murthy: cofounder of Infosys, the second largest information technology company in India
- Vinod Khosla: cofounder of Sun Microsystems, a computer systems and software company
- Anurag Dikshit: cofounder of PartyGaming, a network of gambling sites
- Sachin Bansal and Binny Bansal: founders of Flipkart, a successful e-commerce firm in India
- Chandra Kintala: vice president of Bell Laboratories, a research and development company
- Sundar Pichai, CEO of Google

All of them are graduates of the Indian Institutes of Technology (IIT).

Nicknamed the MIT (Massachusetts Institute of Technology) of India, IIT is a highly competitive public university made up of twenty-three campuses throughout India. The number of students at individual campuses ranges from fewer than 200 to about 6,500.

It's not easy to get into IIT. The entrance exam, IIT Joint

(continued on the next page)

(continued from the previous page)

Entrance Exam (IIT-JEE), is so challenging that schools that prepare students for it are quite popular. More than 90 percent of students who pass the IIT-JEE have taken an exam coaching class. Vinod Khosla says that IIT is one of the hardest schools to get into in the world. Think of a university with the best of what Harvard, MIT, and Princeton have to offer. That's how India thinks of IIT.

But the school has critics. Some worry that too many graduates head to the United States and elsewhere overseas for more advanced education. At one time, as many as 70 percent of IIT graduates left India for other countries. That number dropped to about 30 percent by 2005 because India's economy improved, making it easier for grads to find work in their own country.

To help cover the cost of airfare from India to California, where Stanford is located, Pichai's father tried to take out a loan. It did not come through in time, so the money came instead from the family's savings. The $1,000 that Pichai used to travel abroad was more than his father's annual salary.

Once Pichai reached the United States, he had trouble getting used to his new country. He arrived at Stanford in 1993 and couldn't believe how pricey everything was. He could not afford a new backpack, so he purchased a used one.

He lived with a host family during his first year in America but desperately missed his girlfriend, Anjali. Neither had much money, and phone calls between India and California cost a lot, so months would go by before they could talk to each other. But Pichai had asked

Anjali to marry him during their last year together at IIT Kharagpur. Anjali eventually joined him in the United States, and they married and had two children.

Pichai had planned to earn his PhD at Stanford and become a professor and researcher. Against the wishes of his parents, however, he decided to leave Stanford with just his master's degree. One usually needs at least a doctorate, which requires several years of study, to become a professor. A master's degree usually takes two or three years.

Like many who immigrated to the United States for higher education in technology, Sundar Pichai attended Stanford University, shown here, for his graduate degree. He'd intended to earn his PhD but left Stanford without a doctorate to quickly enter the workforce.

Pichai took a job as an engineer and product manager with Applied Materials, a company that makes semiconductors, objects that let electricity move through them. Pichai also earned a graduate degree in business from the University of Pennsylvania's Wharton School. He worked as a consultant, or adviser, at McKinsey and Company. His combination of technical and business skills turned out to be the foundation for his amazing career.

GOOGLE

On April 1, 2004, Pichai interviewed for a job at Google. This was the very day that Google launched its free email service, Gmail. Pichai wondered how a company could provide such an important service completely free of charge. In fact, he thought it was an April Fool's Day joke. Of course, it wasn't.

Pichai got the job. His first assignment was to join the team working on Google's search toolbar. In this position, Pichai had a relatively low-level role, but it allowed him to use his talent at a

Sundar Pichai met Anjali, the woman who would become his wife, when they were students together at ITT. Here they are, years later in 2016, at the final state dinner hosted by President Barack Obama and First Lady Michelle Obama.

company known for encouraging innovation, or new ways of doing things. So Pichai proposed that Google build its own web browser. A web browser is a computer software application that is used to retrieve information from the World Wide Web. At the time, Pichai's suggestion seemed ridiculous to many. After all, Internet Explorer, Firefox, and Safari were all giants in the market. But Google went forward with Pichai's idea and developed and launched web browser Google Chrome in 2008. Chrome now occupies more than 50 percent of the browser market for phones and desktops—more than Internet Explorer, Firefox, and Safari combined.

Pichai also played a major role in the development of the Chrome operating system (O/S) that runs Chromebooks. An operating system is software that supports a computer's basic functions. Compared to other laptops, Chromebooks are inexpensive, so they are doing well in a market where Windows PCs and Apple Macs once ruled. Chromebooks are especially popular in the education market.

After Chrome launched, Pichai was promoted to vice president and then to senior vice president in 2011. In this new position, he oversaw Google's apps including Gmail, Calendar, Docs, and Drive as well as the Chrome browser and O/S. In 2013, Pichai's responsibilities expanded when he took charge of Android, the most popular smartphone O/S in the world. Larry Page, his boss and a cofounder of Google said Pichai "has deep technical expertise, a great product eye, and tremendous entrepreneurial flair. This is a rare combination; which makes him a great leader."[6]

A great leader indeed. On August 10, 2015, Google announced that the company was being restructured and Alphabet, Inc., would serve as its parent company. In addition, Sundar Pichai would serve as CEO, effective on October 2, 2015. In eleven short years, Pichai had made his way from entry-level management to running the entire company.

GOOGLE

A large multinational company, Google got its start after two Stanford University graduate students, Sergey Brin (chapter 2) and Larry Page, met in 1995. They worked together the next year on a project that would become the Google search engine. Search engines allow users to surf the internet.

Brin and Page had a tough time getting investors to fund the development of their idea but managed to scrounge up enough money to start Google in 1998. In the beginning, they ran the company out of a garage. During their early years, the search engine competed with AltaVista, Yahoo!, Excite, and Lycos. Google overtook its rivals so decisively that now many people use the word "google" as a verb to mean searching for information online.

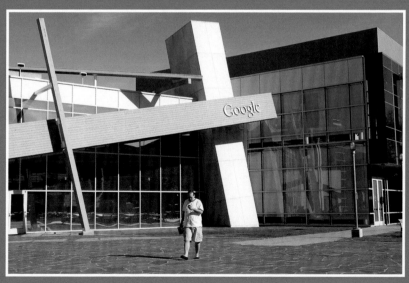

The corporate headquarters of Google are in Mountain View, California. Google is one of many high-tech firms in Mountain View. Others include Symantec, Microsoft, Intuit, Samsung, and LinkedIn. Google is by far the main employer in Mountain View.

WHAT'S RESPONSIBLE FOR SUNDAR PICHAI'S SUCCESS?

No one thing should get the credit, but Pichai has a number of traits that helped him rise to the top. First, he's smart, hardworking, focused, and an expert in his field. In fact, Pichai's master's degree in materials science and engineering trained him to deal with the physical features and building blocks of computers. He learned about molecular mechanics, semiconductors, and materials that might make good semiconductors. Unlike many computer scientists, Pichai understands hardware (the physical components of computers) in addition to software (computer programming and data). Plus, Pichai also understands business and management.

Second, Pichai has the personal characteristics required for success and effective leadership. Christopher Sacca, formerly the head of special initiatives at Google said of Pichai, "He certainly has close friends but he is not political. Everyone knows where they stand with Sundar, and they aren't worried about watching their backs."[7]

Caesar Sengupta, a Google vice president who has worked with Pichai for eight years said, "I would challenge you to find anyone at Google who doesn't like Sundar or who thinks Sundar is a jerk."[8]

Pichai also has a clear vision of why he does his work—a larger purpose. According to Larry Page, "Sundar has a talent for creating products that are technically excellent yet easy to use."[9] Pichai has explained that he wanted to work for Google because he believes the internet works the same for everyone.

"I've always been struck by the fact that Google search worked the same, as long as you had access to a computer with connectivity, if you're a rural kid anywhere or a professor at Stanford or Harvard," he said.[10] He added that it is important "not to just build technology for a certain segment."[11]

Finally, Pichai has not forgotten his humble roots. He remembers how much his parents gave up for him and the hard work parents generally do for their children. "My dad and mom did what a lot of parents did at the time," he said. "They sacrificed a lot of their life and used a lot of their disposable income to make sure their children were educated."[12]

To thank them, Pichai bought his parents a luxury apartment, but they said they prefer the home where he and his brother grew up. Pichai does get to spoil his parents at times. They spend half of the year with him and his family in their California home.

CHAPTER 2

SERGEY BRIN: COFOUNDER OF GOOGLE

O n January 30, 2017, about two thousand employees walked out of work at more than seven offices of Alphabet, the parent company of Google. Their walkout was in protest of President Trump's executive order banning immigration from seven majority-Muslim countries. Sergey Brin, one of the founders of Google, spoke to the crowd.

"I came here to the US at age six with my family from the Soviet Union, which at the time, was the greatest enemy the US had, maybe it still is in some form," Brin said. "It was a dire period, the Cold War, as some people remember it. And even then, the United States had the courage to take me and my family in as refugees."[1]

THE MOVE TO THE UNITED STATES

Born in 1973 in Moscow, Russia, Sergey Brin left the Soviet Union with his family in 1979 in search of a better life. The Brin family is Jewish and faced discrimination and persecution in the Soviet Union as a result. Michael Brin, Sergey's father, had wanted to be an astronomer but gave up his dream before he even started college because the Communist Party of the Soviet Union did not let Jews into physics departments. The excuse the government gave

Sergey Brin is one of the founders of Google. He is shown here wearing Google Glass, which combines eyeglasses with a computer.

for banning Jews from physics programs was that "they" could not be trusted with nuclear rocket research. Since astronomy is an area of physics, Michael Brin could not pursue this topic. He decided to study mathematics instead.

In his new field, Michael Brin continued to face challenges. He wanted to go to Moscow State, a great university that had some of the brightest mathematicians in the world on staff. Like other students,

Sergey Brin was born in Moscow, Russia, when it was still part of the Soviet Union. Shown here is a view of the Kremlin, the base of the Russian federation's government. The Kremlin is basically the "White House" of Russia.

Michael had to take entrance exams. But unlike others, Jewish students were tested in separate exam rooms and graded more harshly. Despite the university's anti-Semitic double standards, Michael managed to get in and graduated with honors in 1970.

He wanted to go to graduate school next, but no one would take him because he was Jewish. At the time, Michael Brin believed this treatment "was normal."[2] So, he continued to study math on his own. He showed up at university seminars, wrote, and published research papers. He even began to write a doctoral thesis, as the Soviet Union once allowed students to earn a PhD without going to graduate school. They just needed to pass certain exams and have an institution look over their thesis. Michael Brin earned his degree in this manner.

Sergey's mother, Genia, faced similar struggles getting her education. But she also managed to get into Moscow State, where she graduated from the School of Mechanics and Mathematics. Their education helped Michael and Genia Brin to get good jobs and live better than many others in Moscow. They had their own apartment and did not have to live in a shared apartment with other families, which was the norm then.

After the Brin family left the Soviet Union, Mikhail Gorbachev came into power. He presided over the dissolution of the Soviet Union into independent federations.

The Brins didn't live in luxury, though. Their apartment was tiny, 350 square feet (32 square meters) in all. They shared the space with Michael's mother, too. Filled with family, friends, and colleagues, the Brins had a good life in many ways, but it wasn't what they deserved.

In the summer of 1977, Michael told his wife and mother, "We cannot stay here anymore."[3] He made the decision after attending a mathematics conference in Warsaw, Poland. At the conference, Michael interacted freely with colleagues from the United States and Western Europe. He learned that his colleagues from the West "were not monsters"[4] and discovered the opportunities and quality of life available outside of the Soviet Union. According to Genia, Michael said, "he wouldn't stay now that he had seen what life could be about."[5]

So, Michael and Genia Brin took the huge risk of applying for exit visas (papers to leave their country). Michael was eager to leave, but his wife and mother needed convincing. Ultimately, Genia's decision to depart the Soviet Union was based on her hope for her son, Sergey, to have a life rich with opportunities. After filing for exit visas in September 1978, both Brins lost their jobs and awaited their fates. Not every Soviet Jew who applied for an exit visa got one. The Brins were lucky. In May 1979, they received their visa to leave the Soviet Union. In the years that followed, few to no Jews could head out. Then, Mikhail Gorbachev came into power and changed the emigration laws, giving Jews permission to leave if they wished. Gorbachev also allowed freedom of religion for the first time in his nation's history.

The Brin family left the Soviet Union in 1979. Sergey was six years old and remembers their departure as "unsettling."[6] The Brins first arrived in Vienna, Austria, where the Hebrew Immigration Aid Society met them. Next, they moved to the suburbs of Paris, France. Michael's mentor, Anatole Katok, found a temporary research position for Michael. Katok also helped Michael get a job in the United States.

MOSCOW, RUSSIA, AND SOVIET JEWS

Sergey Brin and his family left their home in Moscow, Russia, in 1979 to journey to the United States. What was it like in the home they left?

Brin and his family lived in Russia during the Soviet era, which began in 1917 with the Russian Revolution. A Communist government took over the country after seizing power from the czar. The Soviet era lasted until 1991 when the Soviet Union fell apart. At one time, the Soviet Union was made up of fifteen countries, including Russia, the Ukraine, Belarus, Latvia, and Lithuania. Moscow became the capital of the Soviet Union in 1918 and remained so until 1991. It is the capital of Russia today.

Moscow has the largest population of any Russian city. It has a lively arts culture rich with museums, theaters, and concert halls. The city is world-renowned for its ballet. It is also home to numerous world-class athletic stadiums and ice rinks. The most successful hockey team in the world comes from Moscow, but sports excellence in Russia is not limited to

(continued on page 32)

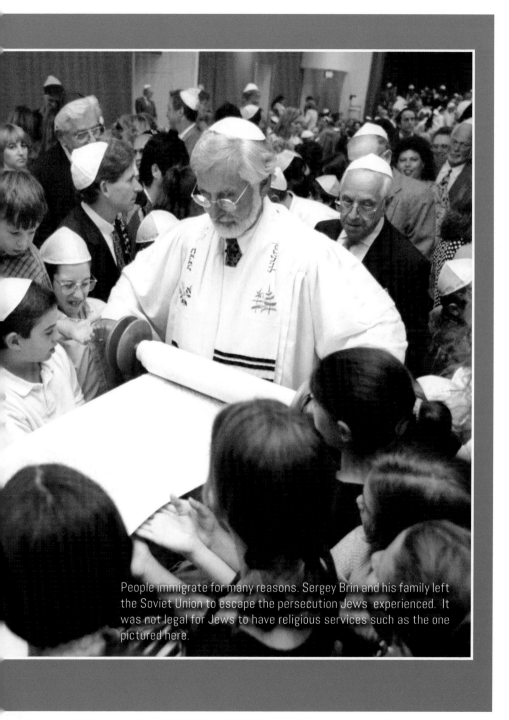

People immigrate for many reasons. Sergey Brin and his family left the Soviet Union to escape the persecution Jews experienced. It was not legal for Jews to have religious services such as the one pictured here.

(continued from page 30)

hockey. More than five hundred Olympic champions of a variety of sports live there.

Brin and his family left Russia because, while not an official national policy, Jews were treated poorly. Conditions were bad for Jews in Russia even before the revolution. Afterward, treatment of Jews got even worse. In 1919, the Soviet government arrested rabbis and seized synagogues and other Jewish property. It also broke up Jewish communities and banned the teaching of Hebrew.

In 1979, it was not easy for Jews to get permission to leave the Soviet Union. When the emigration policy became less strict in the late 1980s and early 1990s, more than half of the Jewish population left to make new homes—mostly in Israel but also in the United States, Canada, Germany, and Australia.

The Brins finally arrived in the United States on October 25, 1979. They found a place to live in Maryland, not far from the University of Maryland. Their first home was a simple cinderblock house, and thanks to a loan from the local Jewish community, they were able to buy a used car. Michael became a mathematics professor at the University of Maryland, and Genia worked as a research scientist at NASA's Goddard Space Flight Center.

SERGEY'S EDUCATION

Sergey's parents enrolled him in the Paint Branch Montessori School in Adelphi, Maryland. He did not have an easy time adjusting to his new world. In fact, Sergey struggled to learn English. Patty Barshay, the director of the school, noted that Sergey "was interested in

Beauty may indeed be in the eye of the beholder. To Sergey Brin, Moscow (pictured) is a drab and decaying place.

everything"[7] but that she "never thought he was brighter than anyone else."[8] She continued to describe Sergey as a little boy who was not "a particularly outgoing child"[9] but one who always had the "self-confidence to pursue what he had his mind set on."[10] Sergey Brin's memories of this time are quite positive. "I really enjoyed the Montessori method," he recalled. "I could grow at my own pace."[11] Sergey's view is that his Montessori education helped to foster his creativity.

Sergey went to Eleanor Roosevelt High School, finishing in only three years. In the summer of 1990, a few months before his

33

seventeenth birthday, Sergey went to the Soviet Union as part of a two-week exchange program for gifted high school math students. His father led the trip. It was the first look Sergey had of the Soviet Union since he left as a little boy. As he observed the drab, crumbling buildings and the sadness on peoples' faces, Sergey had a glimpse of the future that might have been his. On the second day of the trip, he turned to his father and said, "Thank you for taking us all out of Russia."[12]

During his time in high school, Sergey earned enough college credits to finish his bachelor's degree in three years. He graduated from the University of Maryland with a major in mathematics and computer science. He won a prestigious National Science Foundation (NSF) scholarship for graduate school. Then, he enrolled in Stanford University's PhD program in computer science and made his way to California.

A TURN IN THE ROAD AND THE BIRTH OF GOOGLE

Brin had planned to earn his PhD at Stanford and was very successful academically. As one of his advisers, Rajiv Motwani, remembered, "He was the brash young man. But he was so smart. It just oozed out of him."[13]

One of the things that attracted Brin to the high-tech world of Stanford was the school's reputation for supporting entrepreneurs. He was deeply interested in computer science and, more specifically, in the problem of data mining. Brin realized that computers and the World Wide Web had led to the availability of a large amount of information that was constantly growing. Data mining is a method to identify, collect, and understand patterns in the piles of information available. But where does one begin?

Sergey Brin did not achieve his accomplishments completely on his own. Larry Page, his friend, colleague, and cofounder of Google, played a key role in the duo's success.

Fate stepped in during the spring of 1995 when Brin met Larry Page, also a computer science graduate student at Stanford. At first they argued and irritated each other. Brin found Page arrogant and obnoxious, and Page felt the same way about Brin. But they soon began to enjoy their intellectual debates and became close friends. They spent so much time together that others often referred to them as "LarryandSergey."

Like Brin, Page was interested in data mining, so they decided to work on ways to manage and get meaningful information from the World Wide Web. Page wanted to rank the importance of web pages by the number of links they had. He viewed these links as "votes," as in the more links, the more important. Brin and Page called their new program Google and tried to sell it. In the beginning, they had no takers, but that would quickly change.

STANFORD UNIVERSITY: INCUBATOR FOR STARTUPS?

Sometimes location is everything. Situated between San Francisco and San Jose, California, in the heart of Silicon Valley, Stanford University is a true incubator for high-tech startups. Consider just a few of the people who went to Stanford and their accomplishments:

- Bill Hewlett and Dave Packard: founders of Hewlett-Packard, an information technology company
- Vinod Khosla, Scott McNealy, and Andy Bechtolsheim: cofounders of Sun Microsystems

- Reid Hoffman, Konstantin Guericke, Eric Lee, and Alan Liu: cofounders of LinkedIn
- Kevin Systrom and Mike Krieger: cofounders of Instagram
- Marissa Meyer: CEO of Yahoo!
- Evan Spiegel and Bobby Murphy: cofounders of Snapchat
- Peter Thiel: founder of PayPal
- Brian Action: cofounder of WhatsApp
- Jerry Yang and David Filo: cofounders of Yahoo!
- Reed Hastings: CEO of Netflix
- Carly Fiorina: Former CEO of Hewlett-Packard
- Sandy Lerner and Len Bosack: cofounders of Cisco
- Larry Page and Sergey Brin: cofounders of Google

Founded in 1891 and ranked routinely as one of the top research universities in the United States, Stanford is also considered one of the world's leading research and teaching universities. Stanford excels in essentially all areas of study it offers. The university has, however, really made a mark in technology and engineering. It has been especially successful in nurturing the development of technological innovation and startup companies. But how has Stanford managed to do this?

Stanford is a great place to launch a business for a variety of reasons. First, the school's faculty members are leaders in their fields, so students get a state-of-the-art education. Second, Stanford has a first-rate engineering and business program. Third, its extensive alumni network allows students and graduates to make professional connections to find collaborators and investors. Fourth, the university has an "accelerator" program that works to develop entrepreneurs. Finally, Stanford is located in the heart of the high-tech world.

GOOGLE GROWS UP

Even though no one appeared eager to appreciate Google's amazing invention, Brin and Page knew they had made a huge breakthrough. Although Brin completed a master's degree in computer science, he suspended his additional studies to devote his full attention to Google. Brin continues to be on a "leave of absence" from his PhD programs twenty years later!

Brin and Page did get some initial investors—family, friends, and some Stanford faculty—and they bought some computer equipment and rented a garage in which they set up shop. Their first "big" investor was Andy Bechtolsheim, the cofounder of Sun Microsystems. He gave them $100,000 to support development of Google.

From there, the growth of Google is hard to believe. Brin and Page began to sell stock in Google on August 16, 2004. The initial price was $85 per share. In November 2007, it was up to $500 per share. Sergey Brin became a very wealthy man worth billions of dollars. The price per share on March 3, 2017, was $849.85. Brin is even wealthier now. According to *Forbes* magazine, he was the twelfth richest person in the world in 2016.

An unexpected result of starting Google in a rented garage was that the owner's sister, Anne Wojcicki, and Brin really liked each other. In fact, they married in 2007 and have two children. She is also interested in information management, in this case information pertaining to health. She is a cofounder of 23 and Me, a company that offers genetic analysis to the public to determine ancestry and health information.

GOOGLE AND SERGEY BRIN TODAY

Google is the world's most popular search engine. In 2016, it received an average of more than one trillion searches per year. Google has also expanded beyond its original focus. In 2006, Brin and Page purchased YouTube, the most popular website for videos submitted by users. In 2012, Google launched Google Glass, a wearable eyeglass-computer. This device has a touchpad, voice control, illuminated display, and camera. While it did not catch on with the public, Google Glass has found applications in health care, journalism, and the military. In 2015, Google was restructured and organized under the new parent company, Alphabet. Sergey Brin serves as the president of the company. Sundar Pichai (Chapter 1) now leads Google.

ALPHABET INC.

Founded on October 2, 2015, Alphabet Inc. is the parent company of Google. The two founders of Google, Larry Page and Sergey Brin, run it. Larry Page is the CEO, and Sergey Brin is president. The company motto is "do the right thing."

Alphabet's umbrella covers a lot of territory: technology, life sciences, investment, and research. Page and Brin established Alphabet Inc. because they wished to expand into businesses besides internet services, which is Google's main focus. They also thought it would make Google's mission simpler if that company did not have to oversee other business concerns.

One of the exciting subsidiaries of Alphabet Inc. is X, originally called Google X. A semisecret research and development company, X is run by Astro Teller, whose job title is "CEO and captain of moonshots." Projects from X include: Waymo, a self-driving car; project Loon, a network of balloons containing wireless routers to deliver internet service everywhere, including remote places with no access; project Wing, which delivers

(continued on the next page)

(continued from the previous page)

packages across cities via flying vehicles that can hover and lower packages to the ground; project Glass, which is a pair of glasses that deliver information on smart phones by voice command; and a smart contact lens that continually measures glucose levels in tears to help people with diabetes.

The goal of X is to push boundaries and make seemingly crazy ideas a reality. The strategy is to not only accept failure but to celebrate it because they argue that failure means you were really pushing, leaning in, to see what is possible.

Besides his work with Google, and now Alphabet, Sergey Brin has many other personal projects. For example, he and his partner, Larry Page, established a philanthropic division, Google.org, which invests in industries that are trying to solve "really big problems using technology."[14] They have invested in alternative energy companies that are trying to develop sources of renewable energy such as wind. They are also supporting efforts to develop safer and more energy efficient cars.

Sergey Brin has also made significant donations to various charities. One close to his heart is the University of Maryland School of Medicine; his mother is being treated there for Parkinson's disease (PD), a disorder of the nervous system that affects movement. Brin and his mother had 23 and Me test their DNA and learned they have a specific genetic mutation that increased their risk of developing PD later in life to 20 to 80 percent (most PD is not heritable). Brin is pleased to know about his risk of developing PD as he ages because it means he can take measures to delay the possible onset of the disease. His attitude is interesting; he sees his mutation as a bug in his personal "code." He also thinks and believes that knowledge is "always good, and certainly better than ignorance."[15]

Sergey Brin's rise has been staggering. He and his family started out with nothing when they arrived in the United States. Grateful for the opportunities he has enjoyed, Brin works hard to give back to his adopted country. Although divorced since 2015, Brin and his former wife continue to run the Brin Wojcicki Foundation, which they started in 2004 to fund projects in health and education and efforts to end poverty.

He has not forgotten about his immigrant background and is especially aware that he came from a country the United States has long viewed as a threat.

"I'd say the risks at the time, letting in these foreigners from a land that might spy on you, learn the nuclear secrets on the back… and there were many cases of espionage, those risks were far greater than the terrorism we face today," he said. "And nevertheless, this country was brave and welcoming and I wouldn't be where I am today if this was not a brave country that really stood out and spoke for liberty."[16]

CHAPTER 3

PIERRE OMIDYAR: FOUNDER OF EBAY

The gap between people so wealthy that they have everything they could want and those so poor that they can't even provide the basics for their families, like food and shelter, is huge. Many factors have added to this problem, especially automation and globalization of the modern world. Automation means that computers now do the jobs that people once did. Globalization means that no matter where a business began, it can operate any place in the world and hire workers from across the globe as well. These changes have led to "premature deindustrialization" in poor countries. The building of most nations has included an industrial period that produces stable manufacturing, or factory, jobs. Such jobs have historically lifted people out of poverty. But a global market has lowered the opportunity to build businesses in poor countries. The people who live there do not have a way to support themselves or their families. So, is there a way to solve this problem?

A universal basic income (UBI), or a guaranteed minimum wage, could help. A charitable organization called the Omidyar Network has invested almost $500,000 to test the UBI idea in Kenya. GiveDirectly, which has already raised almost $30 million for this effort, runs this program, a twelve-year study. The plan is to

Kenya, shown here, is a developing country where many people struggle to meet their families' basic needs. Pierre Omidyar, billionaire founder of eBay, is using his wealth to help people take care of themselves.

give cash, with nothing expected in return, to more than twenty-six thousand people in two hundred villages. The payments are seventy-five cents per day, which is approximately half of the average daily adult income in rural Kenya.

There are already positive outcomes. Some people have started small businesses, sent their children to school, or made necessary home repairs. Drug and alcohol use has declined in the communities, as has stress. People are more self-sufficient, which means they need

Pierre Omidyar is shown here in 2007 speaking at a conference in Boston, Massachusetts. Three years later, Omidyar and forty other billionaires made a pledge to give away at least half of their wealth in service to others.

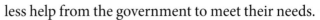

less help from the government to meet their needs.

Investment in the UBI project is one of Pierre Omidyar's many philanthropic interests. He is cofounder, with his wife Pam, of the Omidyar Network. A billionaire by age thirty-one, Omidyar has pledged to donate 99 percent of his wealth to projects that aim to end poverty, improve education, support human rights, and aid in disaster relief. The Omidyars have already contributed more than $1 billion.

Who is Pierre Omidyar and how did he earn so much money, so quickly?

EARLY YEARS AND EDUCATION

Pierre Omidyar was born June 21, 1967, in Paris, France. His parents, who were immigrants from Iran, named him Parviz, but he uses Pierre as his first name.

His grandparents sent his parents to France from Iran to attend college. Pierre's mother, Elahe Mir-Djalali, earned her doctorate in linguistics at the Sorbonne, one of the best universities in Europe. Today, she is a well-respected scholar, while Pierre's father is a surgeon. Because the family is very private, they choose not to make the name of Pierre's father public.

When Pierre was six years old, the Omidyar family moved to the United States because his father had a residency at the Johns Hopkins University Medical Center. Pierre's parents separated when he was a little boy, but he speaks lovingly about their strong influence on him. Both of his parents remained important parts of his life.

IRANIAN DIASPORA

Many Americans think that the United States is the main destination for immigrants around the globe. While it is true that many people do see the United States as a land of opportunity and thus a desirable place to begin a new life, immigrants make new homes all over the world. Let's consider the Iranian Diaspora: Iranian people living outside of Iran and their children born outside of their home country.

Iranian immigrants live in North America, Europe, Persian Gulf nations, Turkey, and Australia, for example. The United States has the largest number of Iranian immigrants if one considers the raw numbers alone. If, however, one looks at the immigrant population in proportion to the overall population size of a country, a different picture emerges. Iranian immigrants make up only 0.1 percent of the population in the United States. The percentages are 0.3 percent in Canada, 0.15 percent in Germany, 0.13 percent in the United Kingdom, 0.15 percent in Australia, and 13.3 percent in Bahrain.

Iranians have left Iran for many reasons. Pierre Omidyar's parents moved to France to

(continued on page 48)

Millions of individuals emigrated from Iran, shown here, to places all over the world, including North America, Europe, Australia, and Persian Gulf nations. The greatest wave of immigration followed the 1979 Iranian Revolution.

(continued from page 46)

pursue their education. They even moved the family to the United States from France because of an educational opportunity. Since 1979, however, most Iranians have left in response to the Iranian Revolution that established an Iranian Republic.

Iran is just one example. People decide to leave the countries where they were born for reasons specific to their circumstances. Some people seek to escape a dangerous or repressive homeland, others wish to pursue educational and economic opportunities, and some wish to have religious freedom.

Because the school Pierre attended in Paris was bilingual, teaching both French and English, he had no difficulty with language when he started school in the United States. Pierre attended school in Maryland through high school, except for eighth and ninth grades when he lived in Hawaii. He attended the Punahou School, where President Obama graduated from in 1979.

Pierre was interested in gadgets from an early age, especially electronic ones. For example, if a calculator broke, he would take it apart and try to fix it (unsuccessfully!). He saw his first computer when he was in third grade. In high school, he would cut gym class to play with the school's computer. This rebellious act actually got Pierre his first "high-tech" job; the principal hired him to write a computer program to print catalog cards for the school library. He earned six dollars per hour.

After completing high school, Omidyar moved to the Boston area to attend Tufts University. He started college intending to major in computer engineering. However, he did so poorly in chemistry (his midterm exam grade was 25 percent), he switched to computer science. Omidyar describes himself as not having been a "good" student. He did not study reliably and though he graduated with a degree in computer science, his overall grade point average (GPA) was 3.01. Omidyar has said that he performed better each semester of college, so he must have had some poor grades early on and then improved. In the end, he learned to program computers.

While in college, Omidyar wrote a program to help Macintosh programmers manage computer memory. Rather than sell it in a traditional way, Omidyar distributed his program online as shareware and asked users to pay on the honor system. He did not earn much but discovered that he had ideas, initiative, and the skills to bring his ideas to life.

THE BIRTH AND GROWTH OF EBAY

After his graduation from Tufts in 1988, Omidyar worked for Claris, a subsidiary of Apple Inc., located in California. In this job, he developed software for the Macintosh. In 1991, Omidyar and three friends started the Ink Development Corp., a software company that wrote programs for the pen-computing market. Pen computers allow users to write with an electronic "pen" that records their physical writing in a computer document. The Ink Development venture failed. However, Omidyar and his friends set up another site, eShop. This was an early e-commerce site, an online place to make purchases. It was so successful that it caught the attention of Microsoft, which ultimately purchased eShop.

In 1994, Omidyar took a job with the software maker, General Magic. He also made money on the side working as a freelance web designer. Once again, Omidyar tried a new business just for fun at first. He put a small online auction service on his personal web page. He called it eBay, meaning electronic Bay, a reference to the San Francisco Bay Area, where he lived at the time. eBay launched on Labor Day in 1995.

Located near its neighbor Google in Silicon Valley, the headquarters of eBay are in San Jose, California.

At first, Omidyar just wanted to offer a site where users could go online, interact with each other, and bid for items. He made no guarantees about the quality of the goods sold, took no responsibility for transactions, and settled no disputes between users.

Collectors of all sorts of things flocked to the site almost immediately. People sold Barbie dolls, Beanie babies, and all manner of household goods. By February 1996, just five months after its launch, eBay was so popular that it had outgrown Omidyar's personal internet account.

Omidyar, along with Jeff Skoll, a friend and fellow computer programmer, opened an internet site suitable for business and moved eBay there. Because this site was more expensive, they began to charge a few cents for users to list an item, and they collected a small fee when items were sold. Omidyar and Skoll had wanted to at least cover their costs. To everyone's amazement, internet traffic to the site continued and eBay was immediately profitable. In fact, so many payment checks were coming in that Omidyar had to hire part-time help to handle them all.

Omidyar realized that he had created not just a profitable business but a community of collectors who enjoyed meeting one another. eBay was making enough money for Omidyar to quit his day job. He and Skoll devoted their time and hard work to building both the technology and community of eBay.

And eBay just grew and grew. Its community doubled every three months. By the middle of 1997, eBay was one of the most visited sites in the world with more than 150,000 visitors bidding on almost 800,000 auctions per day. The average eBay shopper was on the site 3.5 hours per month. It was getting too big for Omidyar and Skoll to handle on their own.

In 1997, eBay received $4.5 million to develop and hired Meg Whitman as the company's chief executive officer (CEO). Whitman transformed eBay into a corporation with a marketing division. Under her leadership, the company also limited the sales of certain items, such as guns and pornography, to separate age-restricted sites. On September 24, 1998, eBay became a public company, which means people can invest in it. On the first day of trading, stock was eighteen dollars per share; the stock price tripled in days.

eBay has succeeded because it's easy to use. Also, it created an online community of collectors, shoppers, and traders. The formula is very straightforward: eBay charges between twenty-five cents and two dollars for each sale listing.

Since going public in 1998, eBay has continued to grow and thrive. By the end of 1998, eBay had 2.1 million members and generated $750 million in revenue, or income. It also expanded, launching new sites in Australia, Canada, Germany, Japan, and the United Kingdom. In 2002, eBay bought PayPal, an online payment processing service. In 2005, eBay opened a new auction category to sell machinery and business equipment. By 2008, eBay was in more than thirty countries, employed more than fifteen thousand people, and had hundreds of millions of customers. In 2015, eBay had more than 265 million transactions during the holiday season alone. Annual revenues in 2016 exceeded $8.5 billion.

THE VAST, WILD WORLD OF EBAY

Launched as a site for collectors to find one another and auction goods, eBay has expanded to become an online shopping/auction site offering an almost unimaginable array of items for bidding and purchase. A list of all item categories exceeds two hundred. Examples of things available include: rare books, antique musical instruments, potty training toilets, forklifts, neon signs, vintage cell phones, wedding dresses, Pez dispensers, bobble-head dolls, lunch boxes, beer-making supplies, boats, motorcycles, tattoo machines, karaoke systems, land, homes, theater tickets, airline

(continued on the next page)

Legend has it that Omidyar started eBay to help Pam, his then fiancée, locate Pez dispensers for her collection. But this story isn't true; an eBay employee made it up to grab the attention of reporters.

(continued from the previous page)

tickets, tarot cards, caskets, and mummified rats. And this is just a sampling.

With more than 165 million active users, eBay has grown far beyond what Pierre Omidyar ever imagined. It has spawned its own "industry" of people posting tips about how to get the most out of eBay as well as statistics about what sells and what does not, so sellers can increase their chances of a successful auction. Businesses even allow people to drop off their goods and let someone else take care of their auction, for a fee.

Amazingly, some people not only earn extra money by making sales on eBay, they even earn enough to quit their fulltime jobs and make loads of money. While roughly a third of individuals selling on eBay make less than $10,000 per year, more than 25 percent earn between $100,000 and $1 million. A small portion of eBay sellers, nearly 4 percent, actually makes more than $1 million per year.

AFTER EBAY: PHILANTHROPY

During eBay's unbelievable rise, Omidyar was also figuring out ways to do good with his tremendous wealth. He and his wife founded the Omidyar Network, a charitable organization that invests in social good. The Omidyars' charity comes from their "deeply rooted belief in humanity"[1] and the "conviction that the world thrives when we prioritize treating others with compassion, dignity, and a respect for diversity."[2]

The Omidyars "believe that people are essentially good, trustworthy, and have good intentions. This was a key belief in the creation of eBay in 1995, and remains an integral part of our lives and work today."[3]

MODERN-DAY SLAVERY

According to the Walk Free Foundation, more than thirty-five million people worldwide are slaves, including many children. Poverty is usually responsible for people becoming slaves. To help support their families or to survive themselves, the poor make "contracts" for jobs and homes with people who have money. These struggling individuals don't realize that they have made a deal with the devil—criminals who have no intention of honoring

(continued on the next page)

Millions of people are living in slavery today. Many of them are poor and become enslaved after trying to make a living. Criminal networks make billions of dollars in the human trafficking trade.

(continued from the previous page)

the arrangement. The poor people get the work but no pay and no way to be free.

Some of the people trapped in slavery are women in domestic service in the United States and elsewhere. Others are unpaid farm laborers, also in the United States and throughout the world. And some are being held captive as sex slaves in various places in the world. According to the United Nations, the entire "industry" of human slavery and trafficking generates $32 billion in revenue per year worldwide.

When Pierre and Pam Omidyar became wealthy beyond their dreams, they decided to do good works with their money. They made ending human slavery and trafficking their focus. They started in Nepal, where the brick-making industry is located; 90 percent of the workers, many of them children, are slaves. The Omidyars initially invested $600,000 to pay for 2,500 children to leave this work and to go to school. They invested additional funds to give the brick workers training in other fields so they could escape poverty.

This was only a start. The Omidyars have donated more than $150 million in an effort to end this horrible practice. They are the biggest private donors to the cause of fighting this terrible industry.

The Omidyars are not going it alone but rather investing in several nonprofit organizations that have been devoted to this cause. Besides helping enslaved people directly, these organizations are also working to pass laws so that slavery can, once and for all, become history.

In 2010, Omidyar joined a list of forty billionaires who have pledged to donate at least half of their wealth. Pierre and Pam Omidyar have also announced their plan for a more extreme goal. They intend to give away 99 percent of their assets over a twenty-year period.

The Omidyars live in Honolulu, Hawaii, with their three children. Omidyar serves on the board of eBay but spends most of his efforts working on projects through the Omidyar Network. His contributions extend far beyond the creation of eBay or philanthropy within the United States—his reach is worldwide.

CHAPTER 4

LISA SU: GAME CHANGER

How do technologists keep up with the latest trends? When Lisa Su, president and CEO of Advanced Micro Devices (AMD), was in graduate school, her adviser encouraged her to "stay technical as long as you can. Once you leave it, you're never going to be able to operate at that same level again."[1] Su took this advice to heart and has followed it by using technology not only at work but in her everyday life, too. Recently, she invited around thirty people over to her home for a holiday party. Su had all of her guests play "Just Dance" on her Xbox One. (This game console is powered by computer chips made by AMD). Everyone danced, earning points by matching their moves to those of animated avatars. Su danced too—her song was Gloria Gaynor's disco hit "I Will Survive".

By Su's own description, "I did pretty well. I had a little practice."[2]

EARLY LIFE AND EDUCATION

Lisa Su was born November 1969 in Tainen, Taiwan. Her family immigrated to the United States when Lisa was two years old. Her parents urged her and her brother to study math and science. Her father, a

Governor Greg Abbott of Texas is trying on the latest virtual reality device developed by Advanced Micro Devices (AMD). Lisa Su (*right*), CEO of AMD, looks on as Governor Abbott experiences a three-dimensional world similar to real life.

statistician (now retired) began quizzing her on the multiplication tables when she was seven. Her mother, an accountant who later became an entrepreneur, introduced Lisa to business concepts. Her parents also gave her three career options: concert pianist, doctor, or engineer.

Lisa Su was born and lived the first years of her life in Taiwan. Shown here is a view of Kaohsiung, a port city in southwestern Taiwan, the region Su once called home.

Lisa clearly believed engineering was the right path for her. "I just had a great curiosity about how things worked,"[3] she recalled. At ten years old, she began one of her first "engineering projects"—taking apart her brother's remote control cars to see how they worked and then putting them back together.

Lisa got her first computer in junior high school; it was an Apple II. Her obvious talent in science earned her acceptance to the Bronx High School of Science. She graduated in 1986.

Lisa's excellent performance in high school made her an attractive candidate for any college. She chose to attend MIT in Cambridge, Massachusetts. Lisa earned three degrees at MIT during her eight-and-a-half years there: a bachelor's (1990), master's (1991), and PhD (1994), all in engineering.

When Lisa started at MIT in 1986, she planned to major in either computer science or electrical engineering. After taking some challenging courses during her first year, she chose electrical engineering because it seemed like the most difficult major at MIT.

BRONX HIGH SCHOOL OF SCIENCE

Founded in 1938, the Bronx High School of Science (Bronx Science) is one of eight specialized public high schools in New York City. To gain admission, students must perform well on an exam that is taken by eighth or ninth graders. More than three thousand students attend Bronx Science, with approximately seven to eight hundred students in each grade. Tens of thousands of students take the entry exam each year trying to get one of the seats in the incoming class. Competition is stiff; the acceptance rate is around 5 percent, but Lisa Su made it in.

Bronx Science is proud of its excellence in science, math, and other subjects. The school has received recognition as one of the best high schools, private or public, in New York State and the United States overall. Moreover, Bronx Science has an international reputation as one of the best high schools in the United States.

The school has had more finalists in the Intel Science Talent Search than any other high school. Eight of its graduates have won Nobel Prizes, more than any other high

(continued on page 64)

Although its entrance may not look especially noteworthy, the Bronx High School of Science (Bronx Science) has a reputation throughout the world as one of the best high schools in the United States. Lisa Su graduated from Bronx Science.

(continued from page 62)

school in the United States. Six of Bronx Science's graduates have won Pulitzer Prizes. Six alumni have received the National Medal of Science, the highest scientific honor granted by the president of the United States; a total of 425 scientists and engineers have received this honor. Of the two thousand current members of the National Academy of Science, twenty-nine are Bronx Science graduates.

Almost all Bronx Science graduates go on to college, many to prestigious schools like MIT, Lisa Su's alma mater.

During her first year of college, Lisa got a job on campus in Hank Smith's semiconductor lab. Semiconductors are essential parts of most electronic devices, including computers. At the lab, she made test silicon wafers for graduate students. Although the job was really grunt work, she did not realize this and thought it was a great experience. Most importantly, this opportunity opened Lisa's eyes to the power and potential of semiconductors. She switched her academic and research focuses to understanding and developing state-of-the-art semiconductor device technologies. Lisa saw a future in which semiconductors are used in most aspects of everyday life.

During her PhD work, Su was one of the first researchers to develop silicon-on-insulator-on-silicon (SOI) technology. When she started this work, SOI technology was an unproved technique for increasing the efficiency of transistors. Transistors are a type of semiconductor device that can boost or switch electrical power or electronic signals. The idea of SOI technology is to build transistors on top of layers of insulating material. When Su was doing this research, no one knew what the practical application of this work

The Massachusetts Institute of Technology (MIT) has a well-deserved reputation as one of the best science and technology research universities in the world. Located in Cambridge, Massachusetts, it was there that Lisa Su earned three engineering degrees at MIT.

might be. Interestingly, SOI technology has turned out to be essential for microprocessors, which are devices that integrate the functions of computers. They are the "engines" that run the computer's operations.

Su's PhD adviser, Dimitri Antoniadis, predicted that she would go far professionally. He noted that in addition to her impressive technical skills, Lisa was also really good with people. He describes her as being a great mentor to other students in his group. As he put it, "She was one of the best students I ever had."[4]

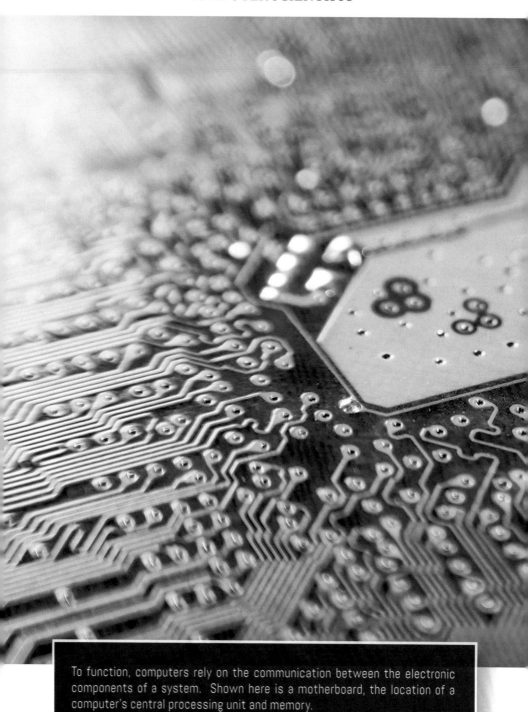

To function, computers rely on the communication between the electronic components of a system. Shown here is a motherboard, the location of a computer's central processing unit and memory.

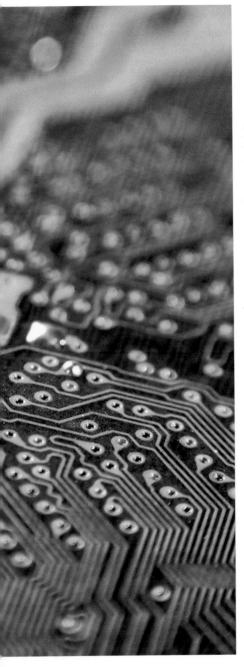

A METEORIC CAREER RISE

After she completed her PhD, Su landed a job at Texas Instruments. Given her experience in graduate school, it is no surprise that she was part of the technical staff of the Semiconductors Process and Device Center. Su stayed at Texas Instruments less than a year because IBM made her a better offer. At IBM, she worked as a research staff member in device physics. She quickly earned a promotion to vice president of IBM's semiconductor research and development center.

While at IBM, Su helped to develop semiconductors with copper wiring used to connect the millions of transistors in a chip instead of aluminum, previously the industry standard. Because copper is a better conductor than aluminum, these chips run faster. A conductor is an object or material that allows for the flow of an electrical current. To make these chips, Su had to prevent the impurities naturally found in copper from damaging the chips during production.

WOMEN IN HIGH TECH

Lisa Su is practically a unicorn in her field because being a woman, a deeply skilled and educated technologist, and a CEO of a technology firm is a very rare combination. She does not have the company of many other women at the level she has achieved. Why is this?

The answer is complicated and the solutions probably even more so. First of all, women account for fewer than a third of people with jobs in scientific research and development. Second, even when women enter a tech-intensive industry, more than half of them leave. In contrast, fewer than one third of men do. In the United States, more than one third of women who earned engineering degrees leave the profession. Only 11 percent of working engineers in the United States are women.

Why do women leave high tech? Again, there are lots of reasons. Most women leave after about ten years in

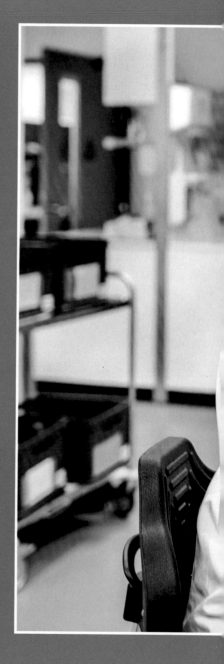

(continued on page 70)

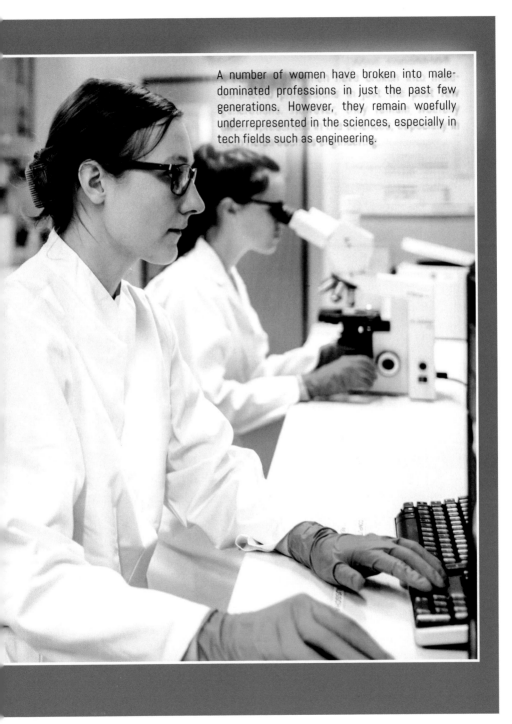

A number of women have broken into male-dominated professions in just the past few generations. However, they remain woefully underrepresented in the sciences, especially in tech fields such as engineering.

(continued from page 68)

the field. What many experience as a hostile, male-dominated work environment and a lack of mentors wears them down. And in the United States, women in engineering, computer, and science jobs are paid less than men.

When we look at executive-level positions, the situation is even more troubling. Forty-one companies on the Fortune 500 list are in the technology sector, and of those, only five have a female CEO. It used to be worse.

It needs to be better.

Su had an interesting approach to the project. "My specialty was not in copper, but I migrated to where the problems were,"[5] she said. In 1998, IBM launched this new copper technology that Su and her team created. In doing so, they produced new industry standards for computer chips.

Su's bosses at IBM recognized her undeniable talent; in 2000 she was assigned to be the technical assistant for Lou Gerstner, the CEO of IBM. She was also appointed the director of emerging products, a position that seems to have been created just for her. At first, this new "department" consisted of her alone. As Su said, "I was basically director of myself—there was no one else in the group."[6] This changed quickly as Su hired ten employees to form what was essentially a startup company within IBM.

Su and her emerging products team had many successes. Their first product was a microprocessor that extended battery life in phones and other small devices. Su also worked out a collaboration with IBM, Sony, and Toshiba to create next generation computer chips for gaming consoles and other purposes. Her team developed the nine processor chip that powered the Sony PlayStation 3, for example.

In 2007, Su left IBM to pursue another opportunity at Freescale Semiconductor. Hired as chief technology officer, she headed the research and development team for two years and then was promoted to senior vice president and general manager of the networking and multimedia group. Su was successful at Freescale, too, guiding the company to a leading market share position in the networking-chip business.

Su's success comes from a combination of talents unusual in one person: significant technical skill and a sophisticated understanding of business. She has managed to continue to grow and develop in both of these arenas. She believes. "People feel like you have to make a choice"[7] between technology research and business. "I find the ability to go back and forth useful," she said. "Sometimes deep technologists find the business strategy stuff boring, but I don't."[8] It is this dual strength that has propelled Su into her most recent and ongoing professional adventure.

RUNNING AMD AND FUTURE VENTURES

Su's successes at IBM and Freescale earned her a reputation as an industry visionary. It was just a matter of time before another high-tech firm provided her a desirable new challenge. In 2012, Su took a position with Advanced Micro Devices (AMD). At one time, AMD was well positioned to compete with their rival Intel, but AMD had fallen on hard times. They were losing jobs and money; many in the field were predicting that the company was going to fail and go out of business. AMD's prospects were grim. They were $2.5 billion in debt and had made a profit only once during the previous five years.

In 2012, AMD offered Su an appointment as senior vice president and general manager. Her first goal was to push AMD to diversify beyond the personal computer market. She led a collaboration between AMD, Microsoft, and Sony to develop and put AMD chips into Xbox One and PlayStation [4] game consoles.

Her initial success at AMD catapulted her into the top position at the company. In 2014, she was appointed CEO and president of AMD. She is one of very few women at this leadership level in the entire high-tech industry.

Su's task was clear—she had to reshape AMD so it would once again be a technology player. She accomplished this goal by making some smart designs. First, she paid attention to the company's culture, how effectively they performed their business functions, and their technology development. Second, she continued the refocusing of the mission to streamline and diversify the company. She decided AMD should choose the correct markets and focus on their strengths. Su defined three specific focus areas: gaming, data centers (like data clouds), and immersive devices (like virtual reality). A data center (or data cloud) is a large group of networked computers used to store large amounts of data. Virtual reality is a computer-generated three-dimensional environment in which users can interact as if it is real. Third, she decided upon a three-pronged approach: build great products, deepen customer relationships, and simplify the business.

SONY PLAYSTATION

First released by Sony in Japan in 1994 and North America in 1995, the PlayStation is a home video game console. When the first version of the PlayStation entered the market, it faced competition

Computer game development and innovation are strong driving forces for technology development, especially computer graphics. Shown here is a gamer wearing a PlayStation virtual reality headset.

from Nintendo 64 and Sega Saturn. By 1999, more than one hundred million PlayStation units had been sold. PlayStation can perform multiple functions. In addition to playing games, it can play audio CDs and some models can play videodiscs as well.

As computer technology improves so does computer gaming. And computer gaming development helps to drive technological advances. There's a connection between the two, especially in the area of graphics and visualization.

The first generation of PlayStation was succeeded by PlayStation 2, which was replaced by PlayStation 3. By the late 1990s PlayStation had overtaken both Nintendo and Sega in the

(continued on the next page)

(continued from the previous page)

game console market. Its continuing success was in large part because of the new computer chips made by Lisa Su's company, AMD, which delivered better speed and graphics.

Sony released PlayStation 4 in 2013 and sold more than seven million units in less than a year. In fact, it outsold its competitor Microsoft Xbox by more than 40 percent; Sony had difficulty keeping it in stock. Despite this, Sony decided to stop developing the next generation of PlayStation because it wanted to move away from hardware-based game consoles. In 2014, it launched PlayStation Now, a streaming cloud-based game service. Users can subscribe to have access to almost five hundred games with more games added weekly. AMD plays a role in this new system, too. They make the processors necessary for the gaming system to work.

Her company vison and implementation of goals is certainly paying off. In 2012, only[10] percent of AMD's sales came from nonpersonal computer (PC) products. By 2015, approximately 40 percent of sales came from non-PC products such as gaming consoles. In fact, AMD is the only supplier of the customized chips that Microsoft and Sony use for their video game consoles. Under Su's guidance, AMD also made a profitable deal to license chip designs in China.

Within two years of becoming president and CEO, Su had turned AMD around. Having lost money for years, the company was profitable again. Its stock has more than quadrupled in price since she took over.

As important as it has been to get AMD back on stable footing, Su is looking toward the future and ways to keep AMD healthy as a company and at the forefront of technology. To do this, she knows she must help engineers come together to design new devices. She is well-suited for this task, recognizing that her key attributes as a leader are having a strong vision, being able to communicate that vision, and knowing how much work it takes to get the job done.

Su envisions that future growth areas for AMD include medical imaging technology and devices and virtual reality. She thinks that developing high-performance computer graphics and visualization technologies can actually change the world. As for virtual reality, an experience in which the user feels drawn into another world, Su wants AMD to be a leader.

"Today there are maybe a couple of million people using virtual reality," she said. "We'd like to see that be 100 million over the next five years."[9]

Given Su's winning track record, chances are she'll achieve this goal.

CHAPTER 5

JAN KOUM: WHATSAPP

On February 19, 2014, Jan Koum took a drive to a familiar building in Mountain View, California. Brian Acton, his friend and business partner, and Jim Goetz of Sequoia Venture Capitalists tagged along. The rundown building that stood before these three men once housed the offices of the North County Social Services. As a teenager newly in the United States, Jan Koum had to visit this building regularly and wait in line to collect food stamps for his family. They were poor and needed government assistance to survive.

On this day, however, he was there for a different reason, one that could not be more different from his experience as a young person. Jan Koum was at the building to sign a contract to sell his messaging app, WhatsApp, for the staggering sum of $19 billion.

How was Jan Koum able to transform his life so dramatically, going literally from rags to riches?

EARLY LIFE IN UKRAINE

Jan Koum was born in Kiev, Ukraine, on February 24, 1976. At the time, Ukraine belonged to the Soviet Union. He grew up in a small village, Fastiv, just outside of Kiev. Koum describes himself as being a "rebellious

Jan Koum, CEO and cofounder of WhatsApp, is seen here at the Mobile World Congress. Koum sold WhatsApp to Mark Zuckerberg, founder of Facebook, for billions of dollars less than a week before this picture was taken in February 2014.

Jan Koum was born in Kiev, Ukraine, while it was still part of the Soviet Union. This beautiful cathedral shows one aspect of Kiev. Koum grew up just outside of Kiev, in Fastiv, in conditions not nearly as nice.

little kid,"[1] and Fastiv as tough and "rundown."[2] His family's home was modest; they had no running water. Koum recalled that his school did not even have an inside bathroom. "Imagine the Ukrainian winter, -20 C =-4 F, where little kids have to stroll across the parking lot to use the bathroom,"[3] he said.

The physical challenges of his school were only one of the difficulties he faced. He didn't grow up with many learning tools. "I didn't have a computer until I was 19—but I did have an abacus."[4]

Jan grew up in a society that kept a close watch on its citizens. He and his family lived in constant fear of the secret police. As Jews in the Soviet Union, the Koum family was even more vulnerable to the invasive powers of the police. And the police did not hesitate to use those powers.

Life was not easy for the Koum family, but once the Soviet Union collapsed in 1991, Jews were allowed to leave. In 1992, a sixteen-year-old Jan moved to the United States along with his mother and grandmother. His father stayed behind but planned to join the family later.

FASTIV, UKRAINE

Once part of the Soviet Union, Ukraine is now an independent country that borders Russia, Belarus, Poland, Slovakia, Hungary, Romania, Moldova, the Black Sea, and the Sea of Azov. It is the largest country, by area, of any entirely within Europe. Its population is about forty-three million. While Ukrainian is the official language, twenty other languages are spoken regionally.

Jan Koum's family came from Fastiv, a city near Kiev, Ukraine's capital and largest city. With a population of about forty-eight thousand, Fastiv is a fairly small city. But the railroad runs through it, transporting people from Central Europe to Russia and Asia. Most residents work for the railroad, but the brewing and machinery industries also thrive in Fastiv.

Like other places in Eastern Europe and the former Soviet Union, Fastiv was vicious to its Jewish citizens. In 1919, the Russian army killed 1,800 Jews; this was probably around 25 percent of the entire population. In 1941, the German army executed all Jews between the ages of twelve and sixty. Even after World War II, conditions did not encourage Jews to stay in Fastiv. The population of Jews in Fastiv in 1905 was 7,095. It was 3,545 in 1939. By 2015, it was thirty-one. Jan Koum and his family were part of a large group of Jews leaving Ukraine for a better life elsewhere.

Jews in Ukraine were heavily persecuted. Here is an image of Jewish men being registered. Thousands of Jews lived in Fastiv in 1905 but fewer than fifty did by 2015.

THE MOVE TO THE UNITED STATES

Jan Koum arrived in Mountain View, a town in the San Francisco Bay Area of California. It was a stroke of luck that he and his family settled there. In 1992, Mountain View was a nice, quiet town with affordable housing. In fact, the family was able to rent a two-bedroom apartment, thanks to financial assistance from the government. Years later, Mountain View and the surrounding areas became the center of the high-tech industry.

Although moving to the United States allowed Jan and his family to escape some of the hardships they endured in Ukraine, life was not easy in their new homeland. First, they were quite poor. Jan's mother worked as a babysitter, and he took a part-time job sweeping floors in a grocery store. He also did not enjoy his high school. He had more meaningful friendships in Ukraine with his classmates than he had in the United States. He thought American students had shallow relationships.

While his early years were challenging, fortune smiled on Koum when he arrived in Mountain View, California, after leaving Ukraine. Koum arrived before the technology boom, which gave him a chance to excel in the industry.

Jan also missed his father, whom he couldn't contact by phone because calling Ukraine was so expensive. Sadly, his father never made it to the United States; he became sick and died in 1997. Jan's mother became ill with cancer not long after they arrived in the United States. As a result, she was no longer able to work to support Jan and her sick mother. A disability allowance helped the family survive. Life was bleak in many ways, and it got worse when Jan's mother died in 2000. He was twenty-four years old and all alone in the world.

BECOMING A TECHNOLOGIST

By his own description, Jan was a troublemaker in high school, barely graduating. He discovered, however, that he really liked computers. Amazingly, he taught himself computer programming and networking by buying manuals from a used bookstore. He read and worked his way through the manuals and then returned them to the store when he was done. He also used FreeBSD's no-cost open source operating system.

By the time Jan completed high school, he was a skillful, self-taught computer network engineer. He enrolled at San Jose State University and had a part-time job to pay for his studies. Koum worked at Ernst and Young, a global accounting firm, where he was responsible for security

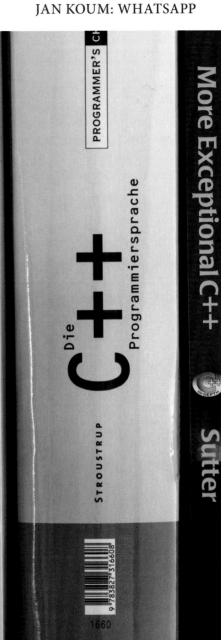

Koum is a largely self-taught computer programmer and network specialist. He relied upon manuals like these to learn.

testing of computer systems. One of his assignments was at the search engine Yahoo! Koum had the duty of inspecting the security levels in Yahoo!'s advertising system. His partner for this job was Yahoo! employee number forty-four, Brian Acton.

Koum and Acton made a great pair. Each had similar no-nonsense ways of working. Both were plain, direct speakers. They

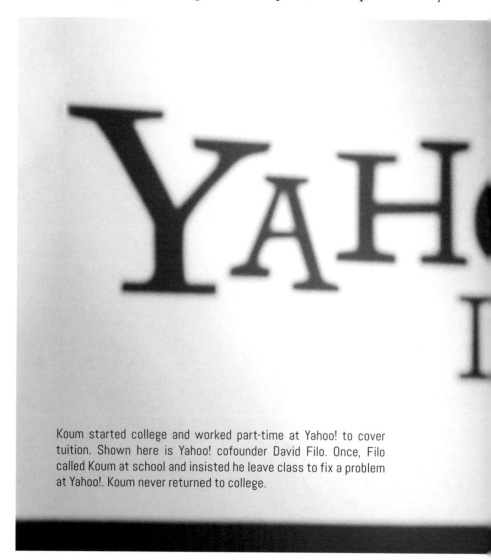

Koum started college and worked part-time at Yahoo! to cover tuition. Shown here is Yahoo! cofounder David Filo. Once, Filo called Koum at school and insisted he leave class to fix a problem at Yahoo!. Koum never returned to college.

worked well together and within six months, Yahoo! hired Koum as an infrastructure engineer. Infrastructure engineers ensure that computer networks run smoothly. He was still attending college at the time but hoped to work at Yahoo! while he earned his degree.

But his plan to stay in college didn't last. Two weeks into his job at Yahoo!, Koum got a phone call while in class. The caller was Yahoo!

cofounder David Filo. A crisis had occurred: the company's servers had broken. Koum told Filo that he was in class, but Filo ordered him to the office. Yahoo! had very few server engineers on staff, and the company desperately needed Koum to help solve the problem. So Koum went to the office and dropped out of school entirely. While he enjoyed learning, he had never liked school anyway.

Koum worked at Yahoo! for nine years, most of the time closely with his friend Brian Acton. The friendship really helped Koum. When his mother died in 2000, Acton reached out to offer support by inviting Koum to his house and going skiing with him. They played a lot of soccer and ultimate Frisbee together, too.

Koum and Acton experienced Yahoo!'s many ups and downs during their time with the company. Finally, in September 2007, both decided they wanted a change. They left Yahoo! on October 31, 2007, and took a year off to travel in South America and play ultimate Frisbee. Koum could afford his time off because he had saved $400,000 of his earnings from his Yahoo! years. Describing his time at Yahoo! on his LinkedIn profile, Koum simply states, "Did some work."[5] His sense of humor didn't end there. His entry also says, "See Brian's profile for more details."[6]

WHATSAPP: "NO ADS! NO GAMES! NO GIMMICKS!"

After leaving Yahoo! and traveling for a year, Koum returned to California not sure at all about his next step. He applied for a job at Facebook but was rejected. He tried to get work at Twitter—again, no luck. Koum still had plenty of money left to support himself, but he knew it would not last forever. Still, having experienced being quite poor, he knew how to live on a budget so the money would not run out too soon.

In January 2009, Koum bought his first iPhone and visited one of the first App stores; it had opened only seven months earlier. Koum had a flash of inspiration. He realized that a new industry was forming right before his eyes: iPhone compatible applications or apps. Generally speaking, an app is a computer program designed to run on smart phones. He decided to get in on this new app market.

But what kind of app did he wish to develop? When Koum worked at Yahoo!, both he and Acton developed an interest in social media, a path that Yahoo! was really not pursuing. Social media refers to websites or applications that allow people to engage in social networking. Also, Koum remembered how difficult it was to contact his family in Ukraine without spending lots of money. He decided to develop an app to make low-cost contact with other people a reality.

Koum kept thinking. He went to the weekly pizza and movie night that his Russian friend Alex Fishman had for the local Russian community. Typically up to forty people would gather at Fishman's home. On this particular evening, Koum and Fishman spent hours in the kitchen talking about Koum's idea for an app.

RUSSIAN DIASPORA

Russians made their first official visit to San Francisco in 1806. Alaska was still Russian territory at that time, and its settlements were without adequate food. Nikolai Rezanov, a high-ranking official in the Russian court, came to buy food for the starving Russian settlers. Rezanov fell in love with San Francisco.

Fast forward to the present. San Francisco is home to a big and vibrant Russian community—around seventy-five thousand Russian-speaking residents. Some of the individuals from this

(continued on the next page)

(continued from the previous page)

population are from families that have been there for generations, and others are recent arrivals.

Russian immigration to the United States, in the twentieth century, can be divided into several waves. The first followed the Russian Revolution in 1917. A second wave occurred during and after World War II in the 1930s and 1940s. A third wave, mostly in the 1970s, consisted largely of Jews. Finally, another wave occurred in the early 1990s, after the collapse of the Soviet Union. Jan Koum's family belonged to this group.

People from the former Soviet Union, even if not actually Russian, are sometimes considered to be part of the Russian diaspora. There are, however, thousands of Jews who left the Soviet Union who do not really identify as Russian. Until pretty recently, Russia (and before it, the Soviet Union) stamped "Jewish" on passports.

Immigrants from the Soviet Union, and now Russia and other Eastern nations such as Koum's Ukraine, found the San Francisco Bay Area welcoming thanks in part to its lively and welcoming Russian-speaking community.

Many people have immigrated to Silicon Valley in pursuit of high-tech careers. Shown here are Russian immigrants meeting with Russian president Dmitry Medvedev during his visit to California in 2010.

At first, Koum planned to make an app that would show the statuses of people in one's phone call list. One could look at the names of contacts and see if they were on a call, if their phone battery was low, or if they were unavailable. Koum named his app, "WhatsApp" because he liked that it sounded like "what's up." He incorporated WhatsApp Inc. in California even before he developed a functional app.

Koum tried to get his project off the ground. He spent a great deal of time and effort creating the programming code to synch his app with any phone number in the world. The early version of the app kept crashing. Koum was about to give up and shared his feelings with his friend Brian Acton. Once again, Acton stepped in to help, this time with plainspoken encouragement, "You'd be an idiot to quit now," he told Koum. "Give it a few more months."[7]

Koum made some changes to the first version of WhatsApp. Whenever users changed their status to say "can't talk, I am at work," for example, everyone in the person's network would get pinged as the update was delivered. Koum's friends started to send updates to each other that were actually messages such as "Running late but am on my way." Koum realized that he had unwittingly created a messaging service and a potentially powerful one at that. Unlike other messaging services, WhatsApp was free and used a person's own phone number as the log in. The number of active users of WhatsApp soared to 250,000 in a short time.

Koum went to see Acton to share his breakthrough. Together they realized that WhatsApp had a lot of potential and decided to take it to the next step. Acton raised money to help them continue their work, securing a total of $250,000 from five ex-Yahoo! friends.

iPhone users liked that WhatsApp could let them text not only friends who had iPhones but also friends using Nokias and Blackberries. Koum and Acton subleased some cubicles and set up shop in a warehouse. They bought Ikea tables for office furniture and wore blankets to keep warm as they worked.

SHORT MESSAGE SERVICE (SMS)

While the ability to send text messages by mobile devices, like phones, was developed in the early 1980s, it took a while to catch on. For example, in 1995, only 0.4 messages were sent per customer per month. Compare that to 2010, where 193,000 messages were sent per second.

The initial technology of texting originated from radiotelephony, the wireless transmission of signals. Short message service (SMS) is a data application that allows phones to send texts to other phones via wireless signals. Approximately 80 percent of all mobile phone subscribers use this service.

Alternative messaging services have entered the market, including WhatsApp, Viber, and WeChat. These services work on smart phones with data connections. More than 95 percent of smartphone users communicate at least once a day using one of these alternative services. WhatsApp is the most popular, for now. However, Viber and WeChat offer some stiff competition. As a result, it is likely that all of these apps will continue to improve, thus delivering even better service to consumers.

At first Koum and Acton worked for free. But eventually Koum's bank account ran low, and they decided to charge users a small fee: one dollar. They improved the app so that in addition to texts, it could send photos, too.

WhatsApp took off; by 2011 it was in the top twenty of all apps in the United States. Venture capitalists tried to invest but Koum and Acton refused to consider their offers, believing that accepting money would mean selling out. One of the venture capitalists did not give up; Jim Goetz of Sequoia spent months trying to get Koum and Acton to listen. His persistence paid off—they agreed to take $8 million from Sequoia if Goetz agreed to act as a strategic adviser and not push to have advertising on WhatsApp.

From the beginning, Koum and Acton insisted on certain guidelines for WhatsApp. Firstly, the app wouldn't feature advertising. The sign on Koum's desk says it well, "No Ads! No Games! No Gimmicks!" He explained, "There is nothing more personal to you than communicating with friends and family, and interrupting that with advertising is not the right solution."[8] Koum further cautioned, "When advertising is involved, you, the user, are the product."[9]

In addition, the app keeps no information about users. In fact, it has encryption between its clients and their server. Encryption converts information into code to protect sensitive or private information. A server is a computer program that provides service to other computer programs.

Last, they have no records of peoples' communications or chat histories. Those records exist on the users' phones but not within the WhatsApp program. All messages are deleted from the server after they're sent.

Koum's motivations regarding these privacy parameters come from his growing up in a country that had a secret police. "Nobody should have the right to eavesdrop, or you become a totalitarian state—the kind of state I escaped as a kid to come to this country where you have democracy and freedom of speech,"[10] he said.

By early 2013, active WhatsApp users grew to two hundred million, and Koum and Acton employed a staff of fifty. Sequoia invested another $50 million to help the company expand. Acton leased a three-story building to house WhatsApp and its growing staff.

SELLING WHATSAPP TO FACEBOOK

By 2012, WhatsApp caught the attention of Facebook cofounder and CEO Mark Zuckerberg. Interested in acquiring WhatsApp, Zuckerberg contacted Koum and for the next two years, the two men met for coffee, dinners, and walks. They discussed messaging and communication services. Koum went to dinner at Zuckerberg's house on February 9, 2014. During this dinner, Zuckerberg proposed a deal wherein Koum would join the Facebook board of directors.

After thinking about the offer for a few days, Koum showed up at Zuckerberg's house on Valentine's Day. The romantic dinner Zuckerberg had planned to have with his wife, Priscilla Chan, was sidelined as he and Koum negotiated their deal while they ate the chocolate covered strawberries originally intended for that romantic dinner. The deal was finalized on February 19, 2014. Facebook purchased WhatsApp for $19 billion.

At the time of its acquisition by Facebook, WhatsApp had 450 million monthly users; within six months, there were 600 million users. WhatsApp continued to grow—700 million users by February 2015, 800 million by April 2015, 900 million by September 2015, and one billion by February 2016. Koum's original goal for WhatsApp was to build "a cool product used globally by everybody."[11] The app is well on its way to that reality.

Koum continues to serve on Facebook's board; he also has stock options in the company worth $2 billion. His wealth has not changed him much. In fact, he tried to hurry the close of the Facebook deal before he missed a flight he'd purchased with frequent flyer miles. This new billionaire did not want to lose the cost of an airline ticket.

Koum also remembers where he came from. One of his first moves after becoming wealthy was to begin to give some of his money away. He donated more than $500 million to the Silicon Valley

Community Foundation, an organization that works with nonprofits to support projects in education, housing, transportation, and civic engagement. Koum also gave $1 million to the FreeBSD Foundation, an organization that offers a free open-source operating system. Koum remarked that he was a FreeBSD user in the late 1990s, and it helped him climb out of poverty because he learned the skills necessary to launch his career.

He hopes his gift to FreeBSD will "lift more immigrant kids out of poverty and help more startups build something successful, and even transformative."[12]

CHAPTER NOTES

CHAPTER 1: SUNDAR PICHAI: CEO OF GOOGLE

1. Rob Price, "Google criticises Trump's immigration order, recalls staff to the US," *Business Insider*, January 27, 2017, http://www.businessinsider.com/google-recalls-staff-to-us-trump-immigration-order-sundar-pichai02017-1.

2. Brad Stone, "Google's Sundar Pichai Is the Most Powerful Man in Mobile," *Bloomberg*, June 27, 2014, www.bloomberg.com/news/articles/2014-06-24/googles-sundar-pichai-king-of-android-master-of-mobile-profile#r=tec-lst.

3. Bharani Vaitheesvaran and Elizabeth Silpa, "The Rapid Climb of Sundar Pichai to Technology Peak: From Schooldays to Silicon Valley," *Economic Times*, August 12, 2015, http://economictimes.indiatimes.com/tech/internet/the-rapid-climb-of-sundar-pichai-to-technology-peak-from-school-days-to-silicon-valley/articleshow/48445105.cms.

4. Ibid.

5. K.V. Lakshmana, "'He's shy, bookish type': Schoolmates on Google CEO Sundar Pichai," *Hindustan Times*, August 11, 2015, http://www.hindustantimes.com/tech/he-s-shy-bookish-type-schoolmates-on-google-ceo-sundar-pichai/story-YJUgz2scaWMsTB3q8hkEhO.html.

6. Brad Stone, "Google's Sundar Pichai Is the Most Powerful Man in Mobile," *Bloomberg*, June 27, 2014, www.bloomberg.com/news/articles/2014-06-24/googles-sundar-pichai-king-of-android-master-of-mobile-profile#r=tec-lst.

7. Sam Thielman, "Sundar Pichai: Google's rising star reaches the top (like his teacher said he would)," *Guardian*, August 15, 2015, https://www.theguardian.com/technology/2015/aug/15/google-ceo-sundar-pichai.

8. Narayan Lakshman, "The Rise and Rise of Sundar Pichai," *The Hindu*, March 29, 2016, http://www.thehindu.com/sci-tech/technology/internet/the-rise-and-rise-of-sundar-pichai-new-ceo-of-google/article7525421.ece.

9. Sandhya K. S. Iver, "Who is Sundar Pichai?," Gadgets 306, March 14, 2013, http://gadgets.ndtv.com/others/news/who-is-sundar-pichai-342476.

10. Sam Thielman, "Sundar Pichai: Google's rising star reaches the top (like his teacher said he would)," *Guardian*, August 15, 2015, https://www.theguardian.com/technology/2015/aug/15/google-ceo-sundar-pichai.

11. Ibid.

12. Brad Stone, "Google's Sundar Pichai Is the Most Powerful Man in Mobile," *Bloomberg*, June 27, 2014, www.bloomberg.com/news/articles/2014-06-24/googles-sundar-pichai-king-of-android-master-of-mobile-profile#r=tec-lst.

CHAPTER 2: SERGEY BRIN: COFOUNDER OF GOOGLE

1. Matt Weinberger, "'Outraged by this order' — here's the speech Google cofounder Sergey Brin just gave attacking Trump's immigration ban," *Business Insider*, January 30, 2017, http://finance.yahoo.com/news/outraged-order-speech-google-cofounder-011736248.html.

2. Mark Malseed, "The Story of Sergey Brin," *Moment*, February/March 2007, http://www.momentmag.com/the-story-of-sergey-brin/.

3. Ibid.

4. Ibid.

5. Ibid.

6. Ibid.

7. Ibid.

8. Ibid.

9. Ibid.

10. Ibid.

11. Ibid.

12. Ibid.

13. Ibid.

14. Cecilia Kang, "Cars and Wind: What's Next for Google as It Pushes Beyond the Web," *Washington Post*, October 12, 2010, http://voices.washingtonpost.com/posttech/2010/10/google_a_vanguard_of_the.html.

15. "Enlightenment Man," *Economist*, December 4, 2008, http://www.economist.com/node/12673407.

16. Matt Weinberger, "'Outraged by this order' — here's the speech Google cofounder Sergey Brin just gave attacking Trump's immigration ban," *Business Insider*, January 30, 2017, http://finance.yahoo.com/news/outraged-order-speech-google-cofounder-011736248.html.

CHAPTER 3: PIERRE OMIDYAR: FOUNDER OF EBAY

1. "Pierre Omidyar," www.Omidyar.com, https://www.omidyar.com/people/pierre-omidyar.

2. Ibid.

3. Ibid.

CHAPTER 4: LISA SU: GAME CHANGER

1. Alice Dragoon, "Found in Translation," *MIT Technology Review*, May 10, 2006, https://www.technologyreview.com/s/405802/found-in-translation/.

2. Wendy Lee, "Visionary of the Year Nominee: Lisa Su, CEO of AMD," *San Francisco Chronicle*, February 26, 2015, http://www.sfgate.com/visionsf/article/Visionary-of-the-Year-nominee-Lisa-Su-CEO-of-AMD-6070002.php.

3. Ibid.

4. Ibid.

5. Alice Dragoon, "Found in Translation," *MIT Technology Review*, May 10, 2006, https://www.technologyreview.com/s/405802/found-in-translation/.

6. Ibid.

7. Ibid.

8. Ibid.

9. Susie Gharib, "Lisa Su Was the Game Changer AMD Needed," *Fortune*, December 21, 2016, http://fortune.com/video/2016/12/21/the-game-changer-amd-needed/.

CHAPTER 5: JAN KOUM: WHATSAPP

1. David Rowan, "WhatsApp: The Inside story," *Wired*, February, 19, 2014, http://www.wired.co.uk/article/whatsapp-exclusive.

2. Ibid.

3. Ibid.

4. Ibid.

5. Parmy Olson, "Exclusive: The Rags to Riches Tale of How Jan Koum Built WhatsApp Into Facebook's New $19 Billion Baby," *Forbes*, February 19, 2014, https://www.forbes.com/sites/parmyolson/2014/02/19/exclusive-inside-story-how-jan-koum-built-whatsapp-into-facebooks-new-19-billion-baby/#2cfe340d2fa1.

6. Zoe Wood, "Facebook turned down WhatsApp co-founder Brian Acton for a job in 2009," *Guardian*, February 20, 2014, https://www.theguardian.com/technology/2014/feb/20/facebook-turned-down-whatsapp-co-founder-brian-acton-job-2009.

7. Parmy Olson, "Exclusive: The Rags to Riches Tale of How Jan Koum Built WhatsApp Into Facebook's New $19 Billion Baby," *Forbes*, February 19, 2014, https://www.forbes.com/sites/parmyolson/2014/02/19/exclusive-inside-story-how-jan-koum-built-whatsapp-into-facebooks-new-19-billion-baby/#2cfe340d2fa1.

8. David Rowan, "WhatsApp: The Inside story," *Wired*, February, 19, 2014, http://www.wired.co.uk/article/whatsapp-exclusive.

9. Víctor Luckerson, "Everything You need to Know About WhatsApp CEO Jan Koum, Tech's Latest Billionaire," *Time*, February 20, 2014, http://time.com/8838/whats-app-ceo-jan-koum/.

10. Zoe Wood, "Facebook turned down WhatsApp co-founder Brian Acton for a job in 2009," *Guardian*, February 20, 2014. https://www.theguardian.com/technology/2014/feb/20/facebook-turned-down-whatsapp-co-founder-brian-acton-job-2009.

11. "Facebook acquires WhatsApp in massive deal worth $19 billion," ABC.net.au, February 20, 2014, http://www.abc.net.au/news/2014-02-20/facebook-acquires-whatsapp-in-$19-billion-deal/5272010.

12. Maria Di Mento, "No. 4: Jan Koum," *Chronicle of Philanthropy*, February 8, 2015. https://www.philanthropy.com/article/No-4-Jan-Koum/151867.

GLOSSARY

app Software designed to run on smartphones.

conductor An object or material that allows for the flow of an electrical current.

data center (data cloud) A large group of networked computers used to store large amounts of data.

data mining A method to identify, collect, and understand patterns in large amounts of information.

e-commerce Online shopping.

encryption A process to convert information into code to protect sensitive or private information.

Gmail A free email service offered by Google.

hardware The physical components of computers.

infrastructure engineer A computer professional who ensures that computer networks run properly.

Iranian Diaspora Iranian people living outside of Iran and their children born outside of Iran.

microprocessor Devices that integrate the functions of computers.

Omidyar Network A philanthropic organization investing in social good.

operating system Software that supports a computer's basic functions.

Parkinson's disease A progressive neurodegenerative disorder that affects movement.

pen computers Devices that transfer writing from an electronic pen to a computer document.

radiotelephony The wireless transmission of signals.

search engine A program that permits users to browse the internet.

semiconductor An essential part of an electronic circuit; it allows electrical current to flow.

server A computer program that provides service to other computer programs.

shareware Computer software made available free of charge.

short message service (SMS) A data application that allows phones to send texts to other phones via wireless signals.

social media Websites or applications that allow people to do social networking.

software Computer programming and data.

transistor A type of semiconductor device that can amplify or switch electrical power or electronic signals.

universal basic income (UBI) A guaranteed minimum payment to help lift people out of poverty.

virtual reality A simulated three-dimensional environment generated by a computer that users can interact with as if it is real.

web browser A computer software application used to retrieve information from the World Wide Web.

FURTHER READING

BOOKS

Beahm, George, ed. *The Google Boys: Sergey Brin and Larry Page In Their Own Words*. Evanston, IL: Agate, 2014.

Bhanver, Jagmohan. *S. Pichai: The Future of Google*. Gurgaon, India: Hachette India, 2016.

Brandt, Richard L. *The Google Guys: Inside the Brilliant Minds of Google Founders Larry Page and Sergey Brin*. London, UK: Penguin Publishing Group, 2011.

Burns, Jan. *Shigeru Miyamoto: Nintendo Game Designer*. Farmington Hills, MI: Greenhaven Publishing, 2006.

Butler, Terry L. *WhatsApp©: How to go From Food Stamps to Amass a Fortune in WhatsAppening!* (Kindle Edition). Brooklyn, NY: Palm Tree Publishing, 2014.

Byers, Ann. *History of U. S. Immigration: Coming to America*. Berkley Heights, NJ: Enslow Publishers, 2006.

Coleman, Miriam. *Designing Computer Programs: Software Engineers*. New York, NY: Rosen Publishing Group, 2016.

Faust, Daniel R. *Building Computers: Computer Engineers*. New York, NY: Rosen Publishing Group, 2016.

Gerber, Larry. *Cloud-Based Computing*. New York, NY: Rosen Publishing Group, 2013.

Green, Sara. *Sergey Brin*. Minnetonka, MN: Bellwether Media, 2014.

Henderson, Harry. *Larry Page and Sergey Brin*. New York, NY: Facts On File, 2012.

Meyer, Terry Teague. *Social Entrepreneurship*. New York, NY: Rosen Publishing Group, 2014.

Mookherji, Kalyani. *Brian Acton and Jan Koum* (Kindle Edition). New Delhi, India: Prabhat Prakashan, 2017.

Porterfield, Jason. *Niklas Zennström and Skype.* New York, NY: Rosen Publishing Group, 2013

Ray, Michael. *Gaming: From Atari to Xbox.* New York, NY: Britannica Educational Publishing, 2011.

Ryan, Peter K. *Social Networking.* New York, NY: Rosen Publishing Group, 2011.

Stewart, Gail B. *Larry Page and Sergey Brin: The Google Guys.* Farmington Hills, MI: Greenhaven Publishing, 2007.

Sutherland, Adam. *The Story of Google.* New York, NY: Rosen Publishing Group, 2012.

Sutherland, Adam. *The Story of Nintendo.* New York, NY: Rosen Publishing Group, 2012.

Swanson, Jennifer A. *The Wonderful World of Wearable Devices.* New York, NY: Rosen Publishing Group, 2015.

Viegas, Jennifer. *Pierre Omidyar: The Founder of eBay.* New York, NY: Rosen Publishing Group, 2006.

Weston, Michael R. *Jerry Yang and David Filo: The Founders of Yahoo!* New York, NY: Rosen Publishing Group, 2006.

White, Casey. *Sergey Brin and Larry Page: The Founders of Google.* New York, NY: Rosen Publishing Group, 2006.

Wolny, Philip. *Google and You: Maximizing Your Google Experience.* New York, NY: Rosen Publishing Group, 2011.

Woog, Adam. *Pierre Omidyar: Creator of eBay.* Farmington Hills, MI: Greenhaven Publishing, 2009.

WEBSITES

Alphabet Inc.

abc.xyz

Alphabet is the parent company of Google and several other companies. Larry Page serves as CEO and Sergey Brin, a Russian immigrant, serves as president. Meanwhile, Indian immigrant Sundar Pichai runs Google. Learn more about Alphabet and the mix of businesses it includes.

eBay

www.ebay.com

Founded by an immigrant, eBay is a place where you can buy or sell just about anything—from musical instruments to clothes to furniture. Browse the wares and learn about eBay's global impact and its history since its 1995 launch.

Omidyar Network

www.omidyar.com/people/pierre-omidyar

The brainchild of eBay cofounder Pierre Omidyar, the Omidyar Network is an investment firm with a charitable twist. It gives money to businesspeople working to create social change in areas such as education, governance, and tech.

10 Years of Growth: Immigrant Engineers in the US Workforce

www.engineering.com/JobArticles/ArticleID/11326/10-Years-of-Growth-Immigrant-Engineers-in-the-US-Workforce.aspx

Engineering.com is a helpful resource for engineers seeking jobs. But the website has also highlighted the contributions immigrants have made to the field in recent years. Learn more about how newcomers to the United States have changed the engineering industry and the countries that send the most engineers to America.

The US Treasury: The Many Contributions of Immigrants to the American Economy

www.treasury.gov/connect/blog/Pages/The-Many-Contributions-of-Immigrants-to-the-American-Economy.aspx

The United States Treasury department is fully aware of how much of an economic boost immigrants have given the country. Here, the treasury highlights how likely immigrants are to start businesses and to help launch new products and services. It mentions eBay, Google, and Yahoo! specifically.

INDEX

ABOUT THE AUTHOR

DONNA M. BOZZONE

Donna M. Bozzone, PhD, is a professor of biology at Saint Michael's College in Vermont. Bozzone is the consulting editor for the Biology of Cancer series (Chelsea House) and author of *Biology for the Informed Citizen* (Oxford University Press). She attended Manhattan College for her bachelor's degree and Princeton University for her master's and PhD, all in biology. Like so many children and, in her case, grandchildren of immigrants, she grew up in New York City.